The Bisley Camp Branch Line

Peter A. Harding & John M. Clarke

M7 class 0-4-4T No. 30056 at Bisley Camp Station on the 14th July 1951. Note the words "Bisley Bullet" have been chalked on the smokebox door.
Pamlin Prints

Published by Peter A. Harding,
Mossgiel, Bagshot Road, Knaphill,
Woking, Surrey GU21 2SG.

ISBN 0 9509414 2 5

Printed by Binfield Printers Ltd.,
Binfield Road, Byfleet, Surrey.

Contents

	Page No.		Page No.
Introduction	3	A Selection of Tickets	24
History of the Line	4	Closure	25
Description of the Route	10	The Present Scene	28
Motive Power & Rolling Stock	16	Conclusion	31
Operation	20	Acknowledgments	32
Timetables	23	Bibliography	32

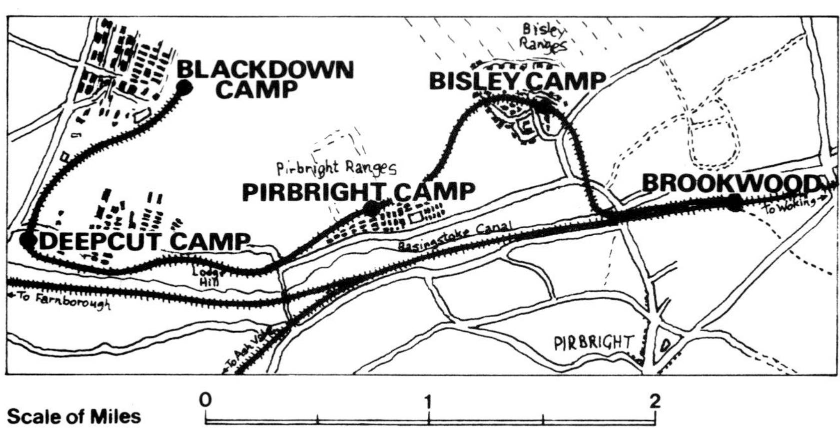

Scale of Miles 0 1 2

Push-and-pull set No. 721 being propelled by M7 class 0-4-4T No. 128 round the curve into Bisley Camp on the 12th July 1947. S. C. Nash

Introduction

The Bisley Camp branch line, which opened in 1890 and closed in 1952, linked the Bisley Camp of the National Rifle Association (NRA) to the main Waterloo-West of England line at Brookwood in Surrey.

It was a short branch, some 1¼ miles long, and was open only for about one month a year to serve the NRA's Annual Meeting which was (and still is) held every July. The line could never really hope to earn much revenue and was only heavily used during periods of national crisis, for example, the two world wars. During the Great War of 1914-18 the branch was extended to connect the huge military encampments which were formed to the west of Bisley at Pirbright, Deepcut and Blackdown.

By the early 1920s the extension had been lifted and the branch had returned to its normal function of serving the NRA at Bisley Camp and continued to do so even though closure seemed likely during the 1930s. However, World War II postponed this fate and the line was once more extended from Bisley Camp, this time only as far as Pirbright Camp.

On returning to peacetime, the branch resumed its normal service and managed to survive until 1952 when it was finally closed.

Today, little evidence remains of the railway and its wartime extensions, but we hope that this booklet will be a suitable reminder of this interesting branch and of the "Bisley Bullet" as the branch train became so affectionately known.

Peter A. Harding & John M. Clarke

D1 class 0-4-2T No. 2260 at Bisley Camp Station during the 1930s. Lens of Sutton

History of the Line

The NRA and Wimbledon Common

The NRA evolved from the war scare with France in the late 1850s. A consequence of this was that Lords Lieutenant were allowed to form volunteer rifle and artillery corps from May 1859. Proficiency in rifle shooting was seen as a fundamental factor in the effectiveness of this force. It was soon realised that a national association for the encouragement of volunteer rifle corps and for the promotion of rifle shooting throughout Great Britain should be formed; so the NRA was established at a meeting held on the 16th November 1859 at Spencer House, London.

The first Annual Meeting of the NRA took place in July 1860 on part of Wimbledon Common which was to remain the site until the NRA later moved to Bisley. The NRA never owned any of the Common, only a small farm which was used for storage of equipment.

For many years the NRA operated a tramway to convey competitors and spectators from Wimbledon Camp to the ranges. The tramway first appeared at the 1864 Annual Meeting and it ran from the entrance at the southern end of the Common to the rear of the firing points, a distance of about 1 mile. The layout was quite straightforward as there were no points or sidings. The track gauge was 2 ft., and six four-wheeled wagons were provided for passengers. These trucks were drawn by horses of the Military Train (the predecessor of the Royal Army Service Corps), with the horses running alongside rather than within the track. The tramway had to be taken up and stored at the end of every Annual Meeting under the terms of the agreement for the NRA's use of part of the Common. Despite the primitive nature of the line, it proved a great attraction and yielded good profits. It is believed the fares were 2d. return and 1d. single, but no tickets appear to have survived.

The horse-drawn tramway at Wimbledon Camp about 1870. Gale & Polden

In 1877, a steam tramcar was placed at the disposal of the NRA by Merryweather & Sons. It was of a boxed-in design, similar to street tram engines of the period, and weighed 4 tons. At the inaugural meeting of 1877, the Prince of Wales was invited formally to open the tramway, and he drove this locomotive along the line. The engine was named "Wharncliffe" after the (then) Chairman of the NRA, Lord (later Earl) Wharncliffe. The NRA purchased this locomotive from the makers in 1878 and it proved capable of hauling six wagons fully laden with passengers.

The NRA, Bisley Camp and the Bisley Camp branch line

In 1888 the NRA was given notice to quit their portion of Wimbledon Common and the search for a "New Wimbledon" began. The London & South Western Railway (LSWR) was determined to ensure that the NRA chose another location within their network. The LSWR's General Manager was authorised to press their case and to offer advantageous terms to the NRA, such as: cheap fares for all competitors, help in constructing the new line, and so on. Several possible sites were considered, but eventually the NRA chose an area of government land called Bisley Common, to the north of the villages of Brookwood and Pirbright. This site had many advantages: it was close to the regular army at Aldershot, it was quite near London, and cheap fares were available by courtesy of the LSWR. Bisley Common was formally approved by the NRA Council in December 1888.

Once the site of the "New Wimbledon" was decided, the branch line which ran from Brookwood (on the main LSWR line) into the Camp was built and opened before all the legal formalities were completed! On the 15th March 1890 the London & Hants Canal & Water Company conveyed the necessary land to the NRA to enable their line to cross the Basingstoke Canal. On the 4th August 1890 the Board of Trade, under the newly passed Tramways Act of 1890, issued the No.1 Tramways Confirmation Order which authorised the construction of the branch as a standard gauge single line (except for a run-round loop at Bisley Camp Station) and the connections with the LSWR's main line at Brookwood. Note that this order was granted a month after the branch was opened by the Prince of Wales on the 12th July 1890. Similarly, on the 17th November 1890, the War Department leased to the trustees of the NRA the right to construct and use a tramway from the 1st January 1890 at an annual rent of 10s. (50p) with 12 months determination by either party; this right was backdated by some 11 months.

The Tramways Act of 1890 explains why the branch was officially known as the "Bisley Tramway". The Light Railways Act (by which the line might easily have been authorised) was not passed until 1896.

The construction of the branch was undertaken by the LSWR with assistance by troops and members of the Royal Engineers in the Aldershot District as authorised by the War Office. The troops were also involved in building the Camp and ranges, and work commenced early in 1890 under the immediate direction of Major J. F. Brown RE. Working parties arrived every day from Aldershot by train, the men marching from Brookwood Station to the Camp. Construction of the branch line proceeded quickly; there were few earthworks of note apart from three bridges: one across the road at the Brookwood-Pirbright arch, a girder bridge across the Basingstoke Canal, and a bridge (which was, in fact, built solely by the Royal Engineers) under the Cowshot Road.

On the 9th June 1890 the General Manager of the LSWR agreed that the railway company would supply the engine and carriages to work the branch in return for half the gross receipts. The line was completed in 4 months, in time for the 1890 Annual Meeting.

The first Bisley Meeting took place on Saturday the 12th July 1890. This occasion was dedicated for the formal opening of the branch, which was performed by the Prince and Princess of Wales. The Royal guests left Waterloo in a special train at 3.30 pm and arrived at Brookwood just after 4 pm. A saloon coach was provided in the train and this was transferred on to the new railway. Here a train drawn by one of William Adams' (the LSWR's Locomotive Superintendent) most recent designs, an O2 class 0-4-4 tank No. 185, stood waiting to convey the guests along the line and into Bisley Camp. The engine had been named

"Alexandra" (after the Princess of Wales) specially for the occasion and was splendidly decorated with flags, bunting, the Prince of Wales' feathers, and the LSWR's coat of arms. On arrival at the Camp Station, the train was met by a huge crowd of visitors. The Royal guests were received by Lord and Lady Wantage and after the formal opening of the Camp and the firing points, the Prince and Princess of Wales inspected the grounds and then took tea in the Pavilion building. Shortly before 6 pm they re-joined their train and left the Camp Station for London amidst much cheering.

When the NRA moved to Bisley, "Wharncliffe" and the wagons which were used on the small tramway at Wimbledon were duly transported and stored at the new Camp. In 1898 the NRA took this stock out of mothballs and constructed a new tramway to convey competitors and spectators from a point adjacent to the standard gauge Bisley Camp Station and, continuing in a north-easterly direction for about a mile, the tramway connected the Camp proper with the otherwise distant "Siberia" ranges. The wagons appear to have been converted from their days at Wimbledon: originally, the seats ran parallel to the track; now, the seats were arranged cross-wise in the trucks. It is not known when the line was last used or what its ultimate fate was.

Soon after this tramway was constructed, another 2 ft. gauge tramway was also laid to transport targets to the "Century" and "Siberia" range butts. Although the section to the "Siberia" butts was later removed, the line to the "Century" butts is still in use and is currently worked by a Lister two-cylinder diesel engine.

O2 class 0-4-4T No. 185 at Nine Elms where it was specially decorated and named "Alexandra" for the opening of the Bisley Camp branch line on the 12th July 1890.

D. L. Bradley Collection

"Wharncliffe", the Merryweather tram engine which worked the narrow gauge tramway from Bisley Camp out to the "Siberia" ranges. This view was taken at Bisley Camp about 1907. Previously, "Wharncliffe" had worked the tramway at Wimbledon Camp. R. C. Riley Collection

Bisley Camp Station about 1912. Note how the station nameboard is on the roof of the building before the main canopy was later added. Lens of Sutton

The later history of the branch line from Brookwood

From the time that the branch line was opened by the Prince and Princess of Wales in 1890, it remained as originally built until the Great War of 1914-18. At the outbreak of the war, the NRA placed its facilities at the disposal of the War Office. This offer was accepted and thereafter Bisley Camp was occupied by regular troops. It became an important centre for small arms training, and in the period August-November 1914 alone, some 150,000 men underwent training at Bisley. This increased activity resulted in a greater use of the branch. The existing Camp accommodation was inadequate so, many new buildings were erected, along with all the necessary stores and equipment; all this material arrived by rail.

As the war continued, other encampments were established to the west of Bisley. This development was typical of sites elsewhere in the country. Some of these camps were linked to convenient main line railways to facilitate the supply of stores, fodder, and to ease the movement of troops. The construction, operation and maintenance of these lines was directed by the Officer Commanding the Military Camp Railways, a wartime development of the Railway Training Centre and the Woolmer Instructional Military Railway at Longmoor.

By 1916, the camps in the Bisley area had become quite extensive and it was decided to extend the Bisley branch to serve these camps. The extension, all on War Department property, was over 3 miles long and linked the camps at Pirbright, Deepcut and Blackdown.

The construction of the extension was directed by the Officer Commanding the Military Camp Railways and was partly carried out by parties of German PoWs during 1916-17. In places, the track was of light spiked construction, typical of other Military Camp Railways and of the haste and urgency in building these lines. The extension was completed by March 1917. The exact date of opening is unclear and confused by the military usage of the railway. Soon after the

This postcard view is described as "Detraining at Bisley" and shows men and troops arriving for training on the ranges during the Great War. Lens of Sutton

Deepcut Camp Station about 1918. Lens of Sutton

completion an opening ceremony was performed by King George V and Queen Mary, both of whom travelled along the line whilst visiting troops in the area. The War Department officially authorised freight traffic as far as Deepcut from the 25th July 1917 and "passengers" throughout from the 1st August 1917. The Bisley Camp branch line and its extension thus became one of several railways operated by the Aldershot Command of the Military Camp Railways. All the camps served by the line were provided with their own stations.

Most of the Military Camp Railways did not survive long into peacetime, but the Blackdown extension lasted a little longer, operating a service of weekend leave trains, until it was closed sometime in 1921. It is not known exactly when the extension was lifted, but this was probably done during the early 1920s.

The NRA's Annual Meetings resumed from the summer of 1919 and during the inter-war period the Bisley Camp branch returned to its normal task of providing a service for their meetings.

Because of the deteriorating state of the track and the ever-increasing cost of maintaining the branch, the possibility of switching the service to the road was discussed in 1932 with the Aldershot & District Bus Co., who were asked to comment. It was eventually decided to retain the branch and repairs were carried out to bring the line up to scratch.

Upon the outbreak of World War II, the NRA again offered the use of their Camp and ranges to the War Office, and yet again Bisley became a centre for small arms training, with the first troops arriving at the Camp in October 1939. Bisley Camp also became the HQ of the Small Arms School for training, experimentation and research.

In 1941 it was once more decided to extend the branch and this time the War Department reinstated the line for about 1 mile, as far as the edge of Pirbright Camp. The extension was almost entirely constructed of spiked trackwork and was contained between low hedges. The date of opening is not known, nor are the dates of closure and removal, but it seems likely that the track had been lifted by 1950.

The NRA's Annual Meetings recommenced from the summer of 1946, along with the railway service. This time the branch was not destined to survive for long. Early in 1952, British Railways Southern Region decided to close the Camp's railway, and the service ceased at the end of the 1952 Annual Meeting on the 14th July.

Description of the Route

Brookwood Station, which is 28 miles from Waterloo, was surprisingly not opened until June 1864 and was partly paid for by the London Necropolis Company who then owned Brookwood Cemetery.

The Bisley Camp branch line commenced from a bay at the western end of Brookwood Station, behind the "up" platform. The bay had its own gated entrance and was separated from the main line platform by high cast-iron railings. A short unloading platform was also provided. Wooden notices facing the bay warned passengers to "Alight on the other side".

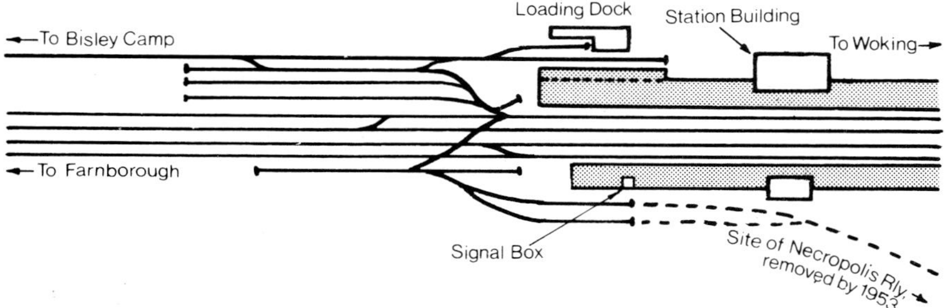

BROOKWOOD STATION

O2 class 0-4-4T No. 232 at Brookwood on the 16th July 1927. H. C. Casserley

From Brookwood the line ran parallel to the main line for a few hundred yards before descending the embankment. It continued for about a ½ mile towards Farnborough before crossing by bridge the road at the Brookwood-Pirbright arch and then veered away from the main line in a northerly direction. Soon afterwards it crossed the Basingstoke Canal over a splendid girder bridge which was laid with check rails and was protected on the far side by a set of cattle grids. Hereafter the line ran through heath and woodland towards the Camp. Shortly before the ¾ mile post the line passed under the Cowshot Road Bridge which, as previously mentioned, was constructed by the Royal Engineers. Several hundred yards further on, the road over Cowshot Common was crossed on a level crossing. This was governed by a 5 mph speed restriction and by "Whistle" boards. Cattle grids were also in use on both sides of the road. A small wooden shelter was provided for a crossing keeper who would show a red or green flag as appropriate. (It is interesting to note, that on all official railway documents, the word Cowshot was always spelt with two t's "Cowshott".) At mile post 1 the line began to curve north-westward at a fairly sharp angle and was check railed as it climbed a gradient of 1 in 50 before entering Bisley Camp Station. Apart from the three bridges already mentioned, there were no other engineering works of note.

Push-and-pull set No. 734 approaching Brookwood while being propelled by M7 class 0-4-4T No. 30027 on the 12th July 1952. The main West of England line can be seen behind the branch 10 mph speed restriction board. D. Cullum

Push-and-pull set No. 735 being propelled by M7 class 0-4-4T No. 30028 over the girder bridge which crossed the Basingstoke Canal en route to Bisley Camp on the 21st July 1951. R. F. Roberts

Push-and-pull set No. 734 being propelled by M7 class 0-4-4T No. 30027 back to Brookwood having just passed under the Cowshot Road Bridge on the 12th July 1952.
Pamlin Prints

M7 class 0-4-4T No. 30027 approaching Cowshot Level Crossing on the 12th July 1952.
Pamlin Prints

M7 class 0-4-4T No. 30027 approaching Bisley Camp Station on the 12th July 1952.
Pamlin Prints

Bisley Camp Station was in the heart of the Camp and consisted of one long brick faced platform and a passing loop. The station building was a modest timber built affair resembling more a cricket pavilion than a railway station and comprised an office, booking hall, and waiting room. At the far end of the station the line crossed one of the internal roads in the Camp. This crossing was protected by cast-iron gates. Just beyond were three sidings which formed the end of the original branch; these lines dealing with coal and other goods traffic. A short unloading platform was also provided at this point.

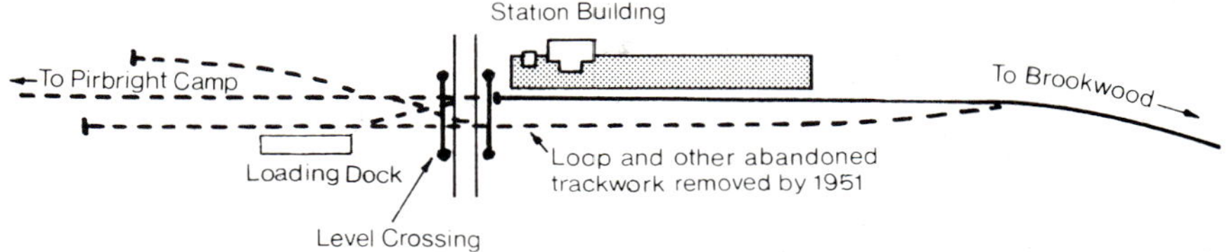

BISLEY CAMP STATION

This view of Bisley Camp Station was taken looking towards Pirbright Camp on the 7th August 1948. R. F. Roberts

From when the station was first built, several changes took place, starting with the extension to the run-round loop in the late 1890s, the platform likewise in 1910 and soon after the main canopy was added at right-angles to the station building. A loop was installed on the far side of the level crossing for use during the two world wars. During the 1930s when all possible economies were being made on the branch, it was decided to stop using the northernmost siding and retain the middle one with a connection from the platform line to serve the south or docking siding. The remainder of the trackwork, including the loop, was then abandoned. Thereafter push-and-pull stock became imperative for the safe operation of the branch.

The route of the wartime extensions beyond Bisley Camp curved further to the west, then in a south-westerly direction, thus almost completing a half turn with the track running towards the Basingstoke Canal. Along this stretch was situated both the Pirbright Camp Stations. During the Great War this consisted of a simple platform, a passing loop, and a short siding. At each end of the station was a level crossing. During World War II the branch was extended again to a point just slightly east of the original Pirbright Camp Station. This time there were two concrete faced platforms and a passing loop. Also at this time, a type of "car port" (a top and no sides) was rigged up for a locomotive. This gave plenty of space to work on a locomotive in the dry.

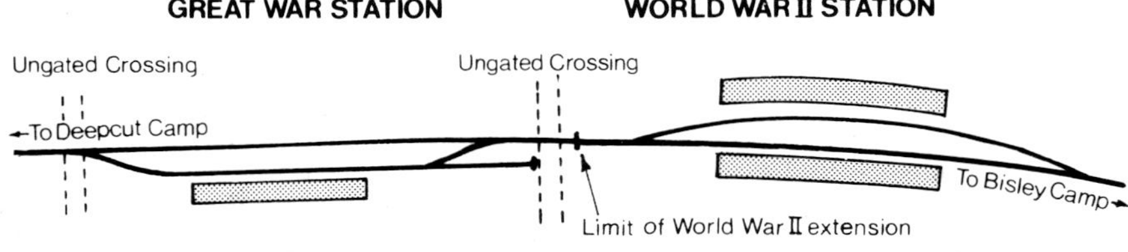

PIRBRIGHT CAMP STATION

Continuing along the Great War extension from Pirbright Camp, the line ran in a westerly direction, virtually parallel with the LSWR's main line, before curving north-westward. As the railway approached Deepcut Camp Station it curved round in a north-easterly direction with the station constructed on the inside of this curve.

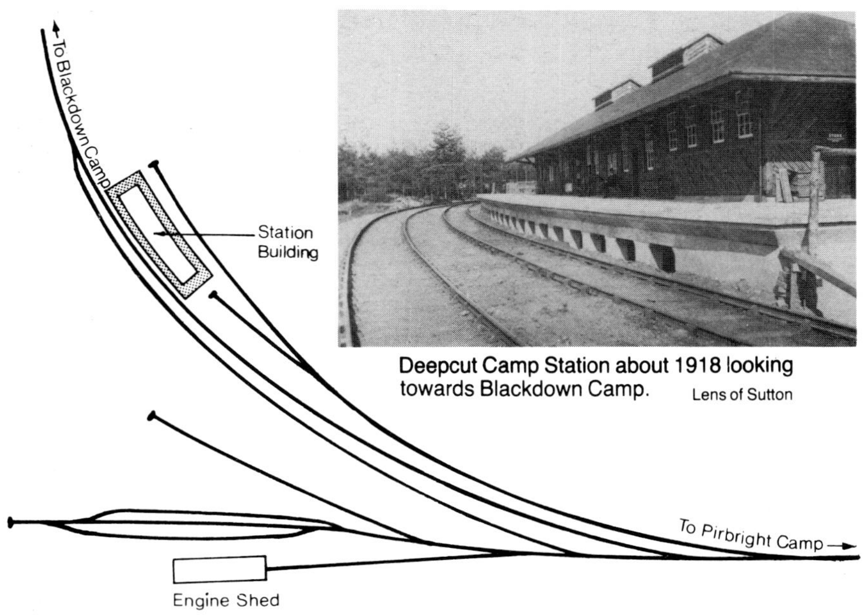

Deepcut Camp Station about 1918 looking towards Blackdown Camp. Lens of Sutton

DEEPCUT CAMP STATION

The station building was remarkable in that it was of a typical log-cabin style. It seems that it was built by Canadian troops in the area, possibly by members of the Canadian Overseas Railway Construction Corps who were under the direction of the Officer Commanding the Military Camp Railways. The building was quite extensive and included a large waiting room, a W. H. Smith bookstall, a booking hall, several offices, and storerooms. On the opposite side of the line to the station was a series of sidings and also a locomotive shed, complete with an inspection pit.

Interior view of Deepcut Camp Station about 1918 showing the booking hall, W. H. Smith bookstall, and the waiting room complete with stove. Lens of Sutton

Moving on from Deepcut Camp Station the line crossed an internal camp road on a level crossing, then continued in a north-easterly direction towards its terminus at Blackdown Camp. Here again there was a platform, a run-round loop, and a short siding.

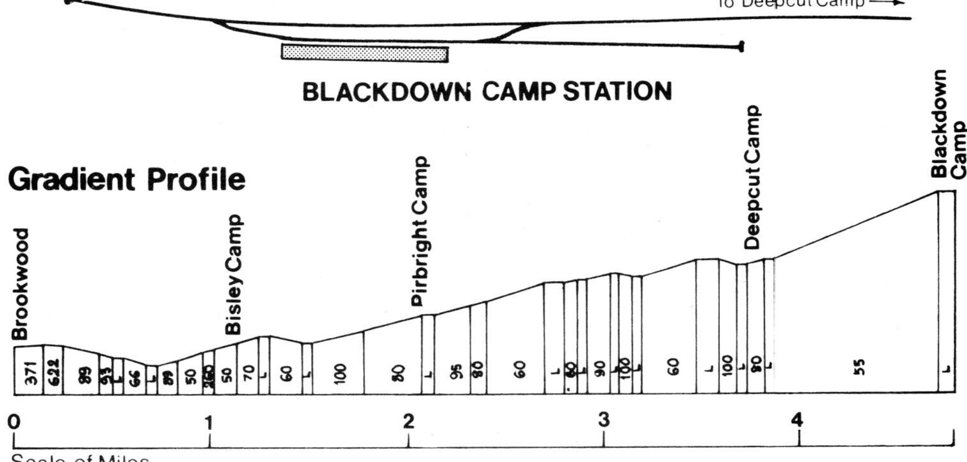

Motive Power and Rolling Stock

When the branch opened in 1890 the motive power was provided by Nine Elms shed and this arrangement was to remain until the summer of 1932, when it became the more logical responsibility of the Guildford shed.

As mentioned in the history of the line, the locomotive which opened the branch was a LSWR O2 class 0-4-4T No. 185 designed by William Adams and specially named "Alexandra" for the occasion.

In 1893, Adams completed drawings of a small four-coupled tram engine for service on the branch but, as the line was only used during the NRA meetings and it would have been difficult to find alternative work for such a small engine with a maximum speed of about 10 mph, it was decided to drop the idea. It is interesting to note that this tram engine would have been quite similar in appearance to "Wharncliffe," the narrow gauge Merryweather tram engine which worked on the NRA's internal tramway systems at both Wimbledon and later at Bisley.

As it was, the O2s were quite able to handle the Bisley Camp branch amongst other duties and in fact they were to work the line up to about 1930. Other individual locomotives of this class known to have been used during this time were Nos 200, 223, 230 and 232.

During the 1930s, the former London Brighton & South Coast Railway D1 class 0-4-2Ts designed by William Stroudley were seen at work on the branch, and Nos B262, 2214, 2260 and 2266 were all thought to have been used on the line at one time or another. From the late 1930s onwards, the branch was worked by the LSWR M7 class 0-4-4Ts designed by Dugald Drummond (the LSWR's Locomotive Superintendent from 1895 to 1912) and Nos 60, 110, 128, 242, 246 481, 672, 30027, 30028, 30056 and 30108 were all seen on duty.

Although the M7s predominated from this time onwards, the line did see an occasional appearance of an Adams 0395 class 0-6-0 and later, because of their greater water capacity in a dry summer, the occasional Bulleid Q1 class 0-6-0 was used.

O2 class 0-4-4T No. 232 at Bisley Camp Station on the 16th July 1927. H. C. Casserley

D1 class 0-4-2T No. 2260 in the bay at Brookwood during the 1930s. Lens of Sutton

M7 class 0-4-4T No. 30028 near the Cowshot Road Bridge on the 21st July 1951. R. F. Roberts

M7 class 0-4-4T No. 30028 with crew, including the guard/conductor (centre), in the bay at Brookwood on the 21st July 1951. R. F. Roberts

During the Great War, with the increased and heavier traffic worked over the branch, it is likely that more powerful locomotives were used for troop trains to and from the Camps.

Once the extension to Blackdown Camp was opened, it became necessary for the Military Camp Railway to station a locomotive on the line from time to time and this was shedded at Deepcut. One engine used for this service was 0-6-2T "Sir John French", originally built for the Woolmer Instructional Military Railway by Hawthorn Leslie & Co. in 1914 (Maker's No. 3088). It is also likely that other 0-6-2Ts from the Woolmer Instructional Military Railway worked the line occasionally along with other locomotives acquired by the War Department for the Military Camp Railways.

World War II saw the return of "Sir John French" then numbered 203 and painted a dull khaki. Another locomotive used during this time was a 0-4-0T Andrew Barclay engine built in 1937 (Maker's No. 2027) and lettered "Royal Navy Whale Island No. 7". This engine was painted in a dark green with red lining.

This view of the Hawthorn Leslie 0-6-2T "Sir John French" was taken at Longmoor during World War II. Aldershot Military Museum Trust

Hawthorn Leslie 0-6-2T "Sir John French" entering Deepcut Camp Station about 1918. R.A.O.C. Museum

Short two-coach sets were used on the branch for the normal traffic worked during the Annual Meetings. In the early years it probably consisted of six-wheel arc-roofed coaches, and later included bogie stock.

After the removal of the run-round loop at Bisley Camp, push-and-pull two coach sets were used. Some sets were ex-LBSCR stock, whilst ex-LSWR gated stock was commonly used for the branch traffic. Sets known to have worked over the line included Nos 363, 721, 727, 734 and 735.

During the wartime extensions, any corridor or non-corridor stock was used for through troop trains. The LSWR stock used during the Great War consisted of six-wheel and bogie stock.

Push-and-pull set No. 721 with M7 class 0-4-4T No. 128 at Bisley Camp Station on the 12th July 1947. S. C. Nash

Push-and-pull set No. 734 being propelled by M7 class 0-4-4T No. 30056 over the girder bridge which crossed the Basingstoke Canal on the 12th July 1952. Pamlin Prints

Operation

Brookwood-Bisley Camp

Bisley Camp was served by railway only during the NRA's Annual Meeting which took place every July. The LSWR (later the Southern Railway and then British Railways) supplied the engine and carriages to work the traffic in return for half the gross receipts.

The normal mode of operation was for a "shuttle" service to operate between Brookwood and Bisley Camp at regular intervals during each weekday of the Meeting (see sample timetables on page 23). Typically, the service ran at half-hourly intervals, with more trains per hour around mid-morning and tea-time. The journey took 6 minutes in each direction, and the branch had a speed restriction of 10 mph. A board stating this speed restriction was situated at both ends of the line.

In the original track layout, run-round loops were provided at Brookwood and Bisley Camp and the tank engine would therefore run round its train of two coaches at each terminus. When the loop at Bisley Camp was taken out of use, push-and-pull sets had to be used over the branch. This also necessitated the application of the single-line rule of "one engine in steam or two coupled" on the branch.

This simple service did vary over the years and, as already mentioned, no trains for the NRA operated between 1915-18 and 1940-45 inclusive. During the years 1919-21 trains ran on Sundays and also on the days immediately before and after the Annual Meeting; by 1922 the service reverted to weekdays only.

The LSWR were quick to offer through trains from Waterloo to Brookwood and even to the Camp itself (see 1909 timetable extract on page 23). This journey took just over an hour. Special fares were levied for competitors: volunteers in uniform were charged 1s. 6d. return (3rd class) as were non-uniformed competitors who produced a NRA voucher. Members of the NRA Council and staff could travel for 3s. return (1st class). These rates were valid only during the Annual Meetings. Usually there were two through trains from Waterloo each year. After the run-round loop was taken out of use at Bisley Camp, an additional engine was coupled to the rear of through trains from Waterloo on arrival at Brookwood and the engine was released only after the train returned to Brookwood from Bisley Camp on the return working.

The branch traffic always required temporary staff at Brookwood. Usually two relief signalmen, two pilots, two guards and two porters were provided to cater for the extra workings involved.

The normal fare charged was 3d. single and tickets were issued by a guard on the train. Volunteers who enjoyed privileged fares from London (as previously mentioned), could make a return journey over the branch for the single fare. By 1948 the fare had increased to 5½d. single. The tickets appear to have been printed by the main line company, and some examples are illustrated on page 24.

The carriage of freight and parcels was authorised by the original Tramway Order. Goods trains were run as required. Latterly freight trains were propelled from Brookwood with the guard's van leading a maximum of three wagons, this being due to the removal of the loop at Bisley Camp.

The Military extensions

During the wartime extensions of the branch, trains were operated by the military authorities and the services were therefore dictated by their requirements – be they troop movements, leave trains, or supply trains. Both "passengers" and freight were carried on the extensions.

In the Great War, tickets were issued at each station and it is possible that through tickets to main line destinations were also issued. The return fare over the extension seems to have been the same for 3rd and 1st class, so it is likely that 1st class tickets were issued to officers only. Some sample tickets are illustrated (page 24) and are of LSWR style and printing.

Specials and incidents

Bisley Camp was the venue for certain events in the 1908 and 1948 Olympic Games. In 1908 the following contests took place at Bisley: rifle shooting, miniature rifle shooting, revolver and pistol shooting, and running deer shooting. These events took place on the three days before the regular Annual Meeting, so the railway service was extended to convey spectators and competitors to these events.

Similar contests were held at Bisley during the 1948 Olympics. This time the service ceased after the Annual Meeting and recommenced between July 26th and August 14th for the Olympic Games. See the special timetable issued for this event on page 23.

★ ★ ★

A remarkable event took place on the Bisley Camp branch in 1939. A special "locomotive excursion" from Waterloo to Brookwood was advertised by the Southern Railway which included a footplate ride over the branch to Bisley Camp. The excursion took place on Sunday 23rd April 1939. It was obviously aimed at railway enthusiasts and over 100 people took advantage of these trips. Probably it was the first time that an offer of this sort was made by a railway company.

The special train left Waterloo at 10.57 am. The fare was 7s. 6d. return which included the journey over the branch. Special tickets were issued for both trips (see illustration on page 24).

At Brookwood, two Drummond 0-4-4T class M7 tanks, Nos 246 and 672, were coupled back to back and with a single coach between them. In this way trains were run at the usual limit of 10 mph between Brookwood and Bisley Camp. Later in the day, a further opportunity to go on the footplate was offered by cut-price tickets.

M7 class 0-4-4T No. 246 with a single coach and M7 class 0-4-4T No. 672 coupled the other end at Brookwood with the special "footplate excursion" between Brookwood and Bisley Camp on the 23rd April 1939. "Lord Nelson" class 4-6-0 No. 864 "Sir Martin Frobisher" can be seen at the far end of the bay platform. F. E. Box. Courtesy of the National Railway Museum

Also in the branch bay at Brookwood was Southern Railway 4-6-0 "Lord Nelson" class No. 864 "Sir Martin Frobisher" with lemaître blastpipe and high-sided tender. The excursionists were granted complete freedom to view this splendid locomotive at close quarters and to "play" with its apparatus and equipment.

In addition, a small exhibition of photographs, prints, and models was on display at Brookwood; whilst in another siding dining cars were provided for refreshments.

"Lord Nelson" class 4-6-0 No. 864 "Sir Martin Frobisher" in the bay at Brookwood on the 23rd April 1939. This locomotive was an added attraction for excursionists who had travelled to and from Bisley Camp on a special footplate ride. F. E. Box. Courtesy of the National Railway Museum

★ ★ ★

On the 11th April 1898 an accident occurred at Bisley Camp Station when the engine of a special train returning the 15th Middlesex Regiment to Waterloo was mis-handled when running round the train. The carriages were pushed back some 40 ft. and with many soldiers already on the train (sheltering from heavy rain, instead of waiting on the platform until the locomotive had coupled up) about 130 men were hurt, 23 seriously, as heads were cut by rifles being jerked out of the luggage nets.

★ ★ ★

On the 4th July 1947, the 3.37 pm passenger train from Bisley Camp to Brookwood struck a Woking Gas Company's van on the Cowshot Level Crossing. The van was completely wrecked and was carried a distance of 50 yards. Two men who were in the van were slightly injured and dealt with at the Military First Aid Post and were later taken home.

★ ★ ★

In 1948 the American Authorities were exhuming bodies of American servicemen buried at Brookwood Cemetery and were allowed to erect temporary platforms on the branch to handle the coffins. The site at which these platforms were constructed was just under a mile from Brookwood Station on the Bisley Camp side of Cowshot Level Crossing.

Timetables

1909 (Summer) Example of Typical Through Trains

DOWN TRAINS

		(A)	(B)	(C)
Waterloo	dep.	1.13 pm	–	–
Woking Junction	arr.	1.49	–	–
Woking Junction	dep.	1.50	–	–
Brookwood	arr.	1.57	–	–
Brookwood	dep.	2.12	2.35 pm	7.00 pm
Bisley Camp	arr.	2.18	2.41	7.06

UP TRAINS

		(C)	(A)	(A)
Bisley Camp	dep.	2.23 pm	6.00 pm	7.25 pm
Brookwood	arr.	2.29	6.06	7.31
Brookwood	dep.		6.11	7.33
Woking Junction	arr.		6.17	7.39
Woking Junction	dep.		6.18	7.40
Weybridge	arr.		6.27	7.49
Weybridge	dep.		6.29	7.50
Surbiton	arr.		6.41	8.01
Surbiton	dep.		6.43	8.02
Wimbledon	arr.		6.53	8.11
Wimbledon	dep.		6.55	8.12
Clapham Junction	arr.		7.02	8.19
Clapham Junction	dep.		7.04	8.20
Vauxhall	arr.		7.09	8.25
Vauxhall	dep.		7.11	8.27
Waterloo	arr.		7.16	8.32

Notes (A) Special with Territorials. Saturdays only when required. Notice given when required.
(B) Special with Territorials after arrival of 1.30 pm Down. Notice given when required.
(C) Empty. Saturdays only when required.

1948 (Summer) Olympic Games and Normal Service

DOWN TRAINS

Brookwood	dep.	8.28 am	8.58 am	Service repeated at same minutes past each hour except 12.58 pm from Brookwood until –	6.58 pm	7.28 pm
Bisley Camp	arr.	8.34 am	9.04 am		7.04 pm	7.34 pm

UP TRAINS

Bisley Camp	dep.	8.37 am	9.07 am	Service repeated at same minutes past each hour except 1.07 pm from Bisley Camp until –	7.07 pm	7.37 pm
Brookwood	arr.	8.43 am	9.13 am		7.13 pm	7.43 pm

Single fare: 5½d.

Notes (1) Train service on weekdays only.
(2) Periods of train service from:
June 28th – July 17th
July 26th – August 14th

A Selection of Tickets

From the collections of G. R. Croughton and C. R. Gordon Stuart

Closure

The Bisley Camp branch rarely made much profit. Under the original agreement between the NRA and the LSWR, the latter worked the line for half the gross receipts. This continued until 1914. After the Great War, the LSWR pointed out that receipts from traffic were insufficient to cover both working expenses and maintenance costs. Thus, no further payments were made to the NRA until the 1930s.

In the years following World War II the branch became more and more of a financial liability and it was decided to close the line. On the 28th May 1952, British Railways Southern Region served notice of their intention to close the branch. Thus the 1952 Annual Meeting was the last served by the railway. By this time the train had been affectionately dubbed the "Bisley Bullet" and its last journey took place on the evening of the 19th July.

A farewell ceremony took place aided by the Gloucestershire Regiment and the Cambridge University Rifle Association. The latter "kidnapped" the winner of the Queen's Prize and escorted him to Brookwood so that he could drive the last train into the Camp. The Gloucesters proceeded to Bisley Camp Station as their Regimental Band played solemn and mournful music. A large crowd assembled at the station to bid farewell to the last train. The engine, 0-4-4T class M7 No. 30027, was adorned with flags, and on the front with two rifles crossed over a target. A speech was made after which NRA spoons were presented to the train crew, the stationmaster at Brookwood, and the superintendent of the Camp station. As the train moved off, a firing party of the Gloucesters fired volleys, and this was followed by a series of explosions caused by a number of fog signals placed along the track.

M7 class 0-4-4T No. 30027 plods through the trees on the curve near Bisley Camp Station on the 19th July 1952, the last day of public service. This locomotive was later decorated for the final run.
The late G. F. Bloxam. Courtesy of R. C. Riley

M7 class 0-4-4T No. 30027 leaving Bisley Camp specially decorated for the last public service journey to Brookwood on the 19th July 1952. The firing party is from the Gloucestershire Regiment. Gale & Polden

This was not the last passenger train to run over the line. Soon after the announcement of the closure of the branch was made known, the Railway Correspondence and Travel Society arranged a special train which travelled over the line on the 23rd November 1952, after the official closure. On this occasion a LSWR push-and-pull set of two coaches, previously used on the Plymouth-Turnchapel service (and then normally used on the Clapham Junction-Kensington service) was used, hauled by M7 No. 30027.

Soon afterwards work began on lifting the track west of the canal bridge. This task was finished by 28th November 1953. The remaining spur was used as a siding for some years, but was later considerably reduced in length before being removed altogether.

The specially decorated last public service train (M7 class 0-4-4T No. 30027) heading up the embankment towards Brookwood on the 19th July 1952. National Railway Museum

M7 class 0-4-4T No. 30027 at Bisley Camp Station with push-and-pull set No. 363 making up the special train which was arranged by the Railway Correspondence and Travel Society on the 23rd November 1952, four months after the branch officially closed. S. C. Nash

Bisley Camp Station on the 23rd November 1952 on the occasion of the special train which was arranged by the Railway Correspondence and Travel Society. S. C. Nash

M7 class 0-4-4T No. 30027 approaching Brookwood with push-and-pull set No. 363 from Bisley Camp on the occasion of the special train arranged by the Railway Correspondence and Travel Society on the 23rd November 1952. John H. Meredith

The Present Scene

The Original Branch

Very little evidence remains of the Bisley Camp branch, and it is becoming increasingly difficult to follow. At Brookwood Station the remains of the bay and the short unloading platform can still be seen, but the trackbed stretching towards Farnborough is now considerably overgrown; it is more obvious from Connaught Road (which runs through Brookwood village and is parallel to the main line). The road bridge by the Brookwood-Pirbright arch was removed some years ago, although the two brick abutments remain. The girder bridge over the Basingstoke Canal survived for many years, but was removed in the late 1970s in connection with the restoration of the canal by the Surrey & Hampshire Canal Society.

The remains of the Bisley Camp branch bay at Brookwood on the 24th November 1985.
Peter A. Harding

The abutments of the former girder bridge which crossed the Basingstoke Canal, looking towards Bisley Camp on the 27th December 1985. Peter A. Harding

Between this point and Cowshot Road Bridge the route is difficult to make out due to new roads, a housing development, and the growth of vegetation. The bridge has been filled in, but from here the cutting remains and the route can just about be made out even though it is very overgrown. Following along the route you come to what was the Cowshot Level Crossing, where today the unsuspecting motorist would never know that a railway once ran across the road at this point.

From the former level crossing, the right of way towards Bisley Camp Station is now an access for a motor car which is garaged just to the left of the route, several yards from the road. As this access is regularly used the former route is easily seen, but from the garage the undergrowth takes over and it is almost impossible to walk from here up to the station.

At the former station it is interesting to find that the platform still remains and the buildings are well preserved and are now the home of the Lloyds Bank Rifle Club. In 1984, the Lloyds Club obtained a former BR Mark 1 sleeping car which now stands on a short stretch of track which has been laid on the track bed. The sleeping car has been refurbished to provide dormitory accommodation for 22 members and was opened with the former station buildings as the official new home of the Lloyds Bank Rifle Club on the 29th September 1984 by Field Marshal Sir Roland Gibbs, Chairman of the NRA and a member of the regional board of Lloyds Bank in Salisbury.

The buildings and platform of Bisley Camp Station on the 28th December 1982, thirty years after the last train had left. Peter A. Harding

The Bisley Camp Station building on the 24th November 1985, now the home of the Lloyds Bank Rifle Club. The BR Mark 1 sleeping car is used as extra sleeping accommodation and stands on a short stretch of specially laid track. Peter A. Harding

The Extensions

The routes of the extensions are difficult to follow and some parts of the line are still owned by the Ministry of Defence.

From the site of Bisley Camp Station the route is easily followed and on leaving the Camp, goes along an embankment in wooded country towards Pirbright Camp.

On reaching the edge of Pirbright Camp the route suddenly comes to an abrupt end. From this point, all signs of the former railway seem to have disappeared although one of the concrete platforms from the World War II extension still survives.

The remains of one of the World War II concrete faced platforms at Pirbright Camp on the 16th May 1964. E. Course

Between Pirbright and Deepcut Camps it is still possible to follow some of the line: just north of Curzon Bridge a section of the route is apparent behind the fuel depot. Further west, just past Lodge Hill, the railway embankment near to the road is still in existence and is now used for access to the canal locks nearby. From here, the line is traceable from a footpath partly on the trackbed and partly beside it which leads through to the Deepcut bridges. Near the end of this path is the site of Deepcut Camp Station, now much overgrown. The large wooden station building survived as offices, stores, an A.T.S. Sergeants' Institute during World War II, married quarters, and finally from the late 1950s until 1970 it housed the R.A.O.C. Museum. When the new barracks were opened in 1970, the Museum was moved into a brand new building and the old station stood empty for some while before finally being dismantled. Nearby, the foundations of the original engine shed can be seen, including the partly filled-in inspection pit.

Beyond Deepcut Camp Station, the remains of the railway and the site of Blackdown Camp Station seem to have disappeared completely.

The log-cabin building of the former Deepcut Camp Station on the 16th May 1964. At this time, the building was in use as the R.A.O.C. Museum. E. Course

Conclusion

For sixty-two years the "Bisley Bullet" served the NRA's Camp at Bisley. The curious limited shuttle service that sufficed for the Annual Meetings was a feature peculiar to the branch; yet the service remained virtually unchanged throughout its years of operation. Looking back, it seems remarkable not that the line survived until 1952, but that it remained open for so long.

Throughout its life the Camp's railway instilled affection and goodwill in members of the NRA and the public who visited the rifle meetings. Many people felt that the last train marked a sharp break with the past, for the NRA's Camps had been served by a passenger carrying railway of some description since 1864.

M7 class 0-4-4T No. 30027 at Bisley Camp Station on the 12th July 1952. Pamlin Prints

Push-and-pull set No. 735 with M7 class 0-4-4T No. 30028 at Bisley Camp Station on the 21st July 1951. R. F. Roberts

Acknowledgments

The authors would particularly like to thank Denis Cullum for the loan of his very informative notes on the line and also to Dick Riley for his help and encouragement at all times.

Many thanks also to the following people and organisations for their kind help in compiling information and supplying photographs for this publication.

Mr. S. C. Nash, Mr. John H. Meredith, Mr. D. L. Bradley, Mr. H. C. Casserley, Lens of Sutton, Pamlin Prints, Mr. R. F. Roberts, Mr. G. R. Croughton, Mr. C. R. Gordon Stuart, Mr. J. H. King, Mr. E. B. H. Chappell, the National Rifle Association, the R.A.O.C. Museum, the National Railway Museum, Mr. I. Wakeford, Mr. R. W. Kidner, Mr. E. Course and Mr. E. Wingfield.

Our thanks to Mr. E. H. Peat for reading the text and to Mr. J. Christian of Binfield Printers Ltd.

Bibliography

THE STORY OF BISLEY: A SHORT HISTORY OF THE NATIONAL RIFLE ASSOCIATION AND BISLEY CAMP by Howard N. Cole.

THE RAILWAYS OF SOUTHERN ENGLAND: INDEPENDENT AND LIGHT RAILWAYS by Edwin Course.

SOUTHERN RAILWAY BRANCH LINE TRAINS by R. W. Kidner.

THE LONDON & SOUTH WESTERN RAILWAY Vol. 2. by R. A. Williams.

HISTORY OF THE NATIONAL RIFLE ASSOCIATION DURING ITS FIRST FIFTY YEARS 1859-1909 by A. P. Humphrey and T. F. Freemantle.

VISIT TO BROOKWOOD (Saturday 9th June 1979) Railway & Canal History Society.

WIMBLEDON AND PUTNEY COMMONS 1871-1971: A CENTENARY RECORD.

L.S.W.R. LOCOMOTIVES: THE ADAMS CLASSES by D. L. Bradley.

THE RAILWAY MAGAZINE (Vol. 84. 1939).

RAILWAYS/RAILWAY WORLD (Vol. 12. 1951 and Vol. 21. 1960).

The trackbed remains of the War Department extension looking towards Pirbright Camp from Bisley Camp on the 7th October 1985. Peter A. Harding